T0049330

WILLIAM SHAKESPEARE'S
AS YOU LIKE IT
A RADICAL RETELLING

ALSO BY CLIFF CARDINAL

Huff & Stitch
Too Good to be True

WILLIAM SHAKESPEARE'S

AS YOU LIKE IT

A RADICAL RETELLING
BY CLIFF CARDINAL

PLAYWRIGHTS CANADA PRESS
TORONTO

Jacket photo by Camille Brodard
Jacket artwork courtesy of Crow's Theatre

Playwrights Canada Press
202-269 Richmond St. W., Toronto, ON M5V 1X1
416.703.0013 | info@playwrightscanada.com | www.playwrightscanada.com

For professional or amateur production rights, please contact:
The GGA
250 The Esplanade, Suite 304, Toronto, ON M5A 1J2
416.928.0299, http://ggagency.ca/apply-for-performance-rights/

LIBRARY AND ARCHIVES CANADA CATALOGUING IN PUBLICATION
Title: William Shakespeare's As you like it, a radical retelling / by Cliff Cardinal.
Other titles: As you like it, a radical retelling
Names: Cardinal, Cliff, author. | adaptation of (work): Shakespeare, William, 1564-1616.
  As you like it.
Description: A play. | Adaptation of: Shakespeare, William, 1564-1616. As you like it.
Identifiers: Canadiana (print) 20220447039 | Canadiana (ebook) 20220447160
  | ISBN 9780369103970 (softcover) | ISBN 9780369103987 (EPUB)
  | ISBN 9780369103994 (PDF)
Classification: LCC PS8605.L5574 W55 2022 | DDC C812/.6—dc23

Playwrights Canada Press staff work across Turtle Island, on Treaty 7, Treaty 13, and Treaty 20 territories, which are the current and ancestral homes of the Anishinaabe Nations (Ojibwe / Chippewa, Odawa, Potawatomi, Algonquin, Saulteaux, Nipissing, and Mississauga / Michi Saagiig), the Blackfoot Confederacy (Kainai, Piikani, and Siksika), néhiyaw, Sioux, Stoney Nakoda, Tsuut'ina, Wendat, and members of the Haudenosaunee Confederacy (Mohawk, Oneida, Onondaga, Cayuga, Seneca, and Tuscarora), as well as Metis and Inuit peoples. It always was and always will be Indigenous land.

We acknowledge the financial support of the Canada Council for the Arts, the Ontario Arts Council (OAC), Ontario Creates, the Government of Ontario, and the Government of Canada for our publishing activities.

For Sage

William Shakespeare's As You Like It, A Radical Retelling was first produced by Crow's Theatre, Toronto, from September 22 to October 10, 2021, with the following cast and creative team:

Writer and Performer: Cliff Cardinal

Creative Co-Conspirator: Chris Abraham
Creative Co-Conspirator: Rouvan Silogix
Associate Creative Co-Conspirator: Ryan Cunningham
Lighting Designer: Logan Cracknell
Stage Manager: Jennifer Stobart
Counsellors: Cheryl McPherson and Jodi Gorham

CLIFF: Hi, welcome to Crow's Theatre's presentation of *As You Like It*, by the great William Shakespeare.
As well, you have the honour of seeing the show with the playwright responsible for the adaptation.
I'm Cliff Cardinal.

    Beat.

To self-identify: I am Lakota, Dene, Cree, and my great-grandfather, on my mother's side, his mother was one-quarter French.

    Beat.

. . . Or Ukrainian.

    Beat.

We're not sure . . . it was a long summer.

    Beat.

The land I'm standing on is the traditional territory of many nations, including the Mississaugaus of the Credit, the Anishnabeg, the Huron, the Wendat, and the Haudenosaunee.
We are trespassing.

    Beat.

We can stay.

    Beat.

Hang out.
Enjoy the show.
Just don't drill for oil.

    Beat.

Don't get me wrong, I love the oil industry.

    Beat.

Did everyone hear me say that? "I love the oil industry."

    Beat.

Crow's Theatre loves pipelines.

    Beat.

Theatre in this country only goes so far without oil money.
You know how far theatre in this country goes without oil money?
The Winnipeg Fringe.

    Beat.

So, I'm not up here going: "No blood for oil."

    Beat.

I'm saying: "*Some* blood for oil."

    Beat.

All right.
But it's not just the drilling.
It's the spilling.
You can't drill without a spill.
For Indigenous people, the Earth is literally our mother.

Please don't spill your hot oil on my mother's coral reef.

Beat.

Better if you just stay seated, in fact.

Beat.

The company has asked that you please turn off your phones.

Beat.

Actually, they didn't ask, I just fuckin' hate phones in theatres.
They piss me off: please turn them off.

Beat.

Let's just be here, together, for a moment, and acknowledge the land.

Beat.

The land upon which we stand is old.
Older than the institutions that gather us today.
The land is older than I am good-looking.

Beat.

Well . . .

Beat.

Maybe not that old.

Beat.

She is the shore that ancient civilizations were founded upon, and so shall
she be the sight of ruins after the last human city falls.

When I put it like that, I'm not too worried about the land.
The land will be fine.
It's us, the people.
With our propensity for extravagant luxuries like . . . oxygen.

Beat.

And water.

Beat.

Not for us.
For our children.
For our children's children.
A long time from now.
Far off, in the distant future.
They say about five years.

Beat.

We'll have the first war over water in five years.

Beat.

Yeah.
I read that.
Don't worry about *where* I read it.

Beat.

Let's get back to trespassing.

Beat.

This stolen land thing . . .
It's a metaphor.
Like saying your prayers.

A story to remind us to be grateful.

Beat.

No.
I'm telling you: the land upon which Crow's Theatre sits was promised to someone else.

Beat.

It's like ... how can I explain ...
It's like someone sold you a ticket to a show.
You get to the theatre, you get to your seat, and you find: someone else sitting in your seat.

Beat.

Simple misunderstanding.

Beat.

You pull out your ticket.
They do the same.

Beat.

Somebody sold them your ticket.

Beat.

You call the usher over.
You explain.
The usher says: "Go fuck yourself."

Beat.

That's the stolen land show.

Beat.

That's a show you wouldn't buy a ticket for.
And now you have to watch.

Beat.

Prime time.
All day.
Every day.
Twenty-four hours a day, seven days a week, three hundred sixty-five days a year, including holidays.
Every Christmas is a white Christmas—
... When you're Indigenous.

Beat.

They asked me to do the land acknowledgement tonight.

Beat.

I fucking hate land acknowledgements.
I find them so goddamn patronizing.
You want me to come out in my beads and feathers and brown skin and bless your event.
Tell you you're "woke."

Beat.

So I said I'd be delighted.

Beat.

But only if we'd really acknowledge.
I mean: I wanna *acknowledge* right now.

Beat.

The first thing I want to acknowledge . . . is that I've seen a lot of land acknowledgements.

Beat.

A lot.

Let me tell you, very briefly, about the first land acknowledgement I ever saw.

The first land acknowledgement I ever saw was delivered by a member of the acting company.

I didn't understand what he was doing at first, but as I realized . . . I thought: "Yes."

Yes.

Someone's finally saying it.

Someone's finally saying what we've been saying back home for a long time, yes.

That was the first land acknowledgement I ever saw.

Beat.

Let me tell you about the second land acknowledgement I ever saw.

Second land acknowledgement I ever saw, and I hate starting stories this way . . . but I start them this way all the time: he was a white guy.

Beat.

. . . And he was the head of a multi-million-dollar institution.

He gave this long, self-congratulating message of reciprocity and account-ability and environmental sustainability . . .

Then he stands there with this far-off look in his eye like he's the last safe house on the Underground Railroad.

Beat.

Follow me to Canada.

Beat.

I said: "What the fuck . . ."

Beat.

He's just gonna roll in, at this late date, and mark himself as some kind of saviour.

Beat.

Then I saw ten million more land acknowledgements.

Beat.

I have seen every type of land acknowledgement by now.
I have been lectured to by students who've only been on the land for twenty years.

Beat.

Can you imagine: being lectured about racism by someone who's only experienced it on the Internet.

Beat.

I've seen first-class one-upmanship:
One land acknowledgement began with an Elder burning smudge, threw to a solidarity statement with an Indigiqueer student group, hit the municipal land acknowledgement, and ended with an honour song by a women's drum group.

Beat.

The land acknowledgement company was bigger than the cast of the show.

Beat.

The show was a classic from seventeenth-century France.

Beat.

Which, if you can imagine, had very little to do with the Indigenous experience.

Beat.

We misappropriated Molière.

Beat.

I guess that's great.
We should think about Indigeneity.
We should acknowledge the land.
We should give Vancouver Island back to my cousins.

Beat.

Shouldn't we?
They do land acknowledgements all the time.
If a five-year-old acknowledges that they stole something, maybe we're not mad, but we make them give it back.

Beat.

I've often wondered what these land acknowledgements accomplish.
Aside from making white people feel good about themselves.

Beat.

Hi.

Beat.

They want me to use this language like: "settler" and "uninvited guest," but I'm just not in for covert racism.

Beat.

"But, Cliff, you can't be racist against white people. You can't be racist against the dominant culture.
"It's impossible."

Beat.

Oh, it's possible.

Beat.

I've done it.

Beat.

You just don't see it every day.
It's a special occasion.

Beat.

What does a land acknowledgement accomplish?
I want my land acknowledgement to mean something.
So here, tonight, by the end of this show—er, land acknowledgement . . .
I'm going to convince you to give your land back to the Indigenous.

Beat.

I swear to God.

Beat.

I'm starting a GoFundMe campaign to redistribute the wealth of the nation to Indigenous people.
The URL is: www.landb—
How come no one is taking out their pens?

Beat.

No, you're not going to give your land back to the Indigenous.

Beat.

We're going to take it.

Beat.

Not through violence.
God no.
Do you know my cousins, the Haida?
They are a litigious people.
They know their way around a courtroom.

Beat.

Go back to sleep.

Beat.

Acknowledge this:
Arts organizations do boring land acknowledgements.

Beat.

This one's okay.

Beat.

A land acknowledgement is a protest.
Protests can be positive; when recognizable action meets broad-sweeping legislation that addresses systemic—you know all this shit.

Beat.

Arts organizations don't care about that.
Arts organizations are here to sustain arts organizations.
Crow's Theatre doesn't want your charitable dollars going to a bunch of
Indians.

Beat.

Don't worry, they're not here.
They're like the Hudson's Bay Company.
They gave us the building and walked away.

Beat.

What we're doing is "spreading awareness."
(spreads like suntan lotion) Squelch.

Beat.

Spread a little awareness here, a little awareness there.
Cuz it's a harsh political climate out there.

Beat.

You gotta spread a little awareness on your—
Oh.
Excuse me, miss, if you'd like, I could spread a little awareness on your back.
In lieu of actually doing something, we're "spreading awareness" and count-
ing ourselves as allies.

Beat.

Sometimes one of these "allies" will come up to me, after the show, and
they'll be like . . .
"What'd you think of the land acknowledgement?"

Beat.

"What did you think of the land acknowledgement?"
What they're really saying is: "Tell me I'm one of the good ones. Tell me I'm one of the good ones."

Beat.

"Would it be so hard to just tell me I'm one of the good ones."

Beat.

When this happens, I lower my voice and say: "There was a protocol you didn't observe . . . and I feel the ancestors are displeased."

Beat.

I say: "Next time, before you begin, hold some tobacco in one hand, face the four directions, and with the other hand, take out your credit card. "Send some money to an Indigenous service organization."

Beat.

A land acknowledgement is supposed to be a protest: a campaign to raise awareness to support Indigenous people.
I mean the environmental movement.

Beat.

Wait, which was it again . . .

Beat.

Am I supposed to acknowledge the land or am I here to acknowledge the Indians?
I'm seriously asking.

Beat.

Is this a protest on behalf of a people who've suffered great injustice or a fragile, interconnected string of ecosystems and biomes.
Indian persecution, or global warming?

Beat.

I like both . . . so both.

Beat.

This is a story of a majestic people who only wanted to live in equilibrium with nature.

Beat.

I don't think our ancestors were concerned with living in equilibrium with nature.
When Crazy Horse drove hundreds of bison over the face of a cliff . . . was it to regulate CO_2 emissions?

Beat.

If you've never seen six metric tons of industrial waste, you don't know the river needs to be protected.
Our ancestors needed the same things we need now: breakfast, love, twenty-four-hour shipping.

Beat.

Our ancestors were less in touch with climate change and evolving ecosystems than we are.

Beat.

Why then, are Indigenous people linked with the environmental movement?

Beat.

There was a poster in my elementary school.
It said . . . I can't remember.

Beat.

But the gist was: a proud, stoic Indian— He was even wearing a Comanche headdress and he shed a single tear.

Beat.

The tear he shed was for littering— Now I remember what it said.

Beat.

"Every time you litter, Gray Owl sheds a tear."

Beat.

I was very moved by that poster.
I considered, for the first time, the cost on the planet and those poor Indians.
I was moved, my eyes were opened—or "woke," if you'd like.

Beat.

It was a magical experience.

Beat.

I was six.

Beat.

If you're an adult and you're like, "Oh, we should take care of the Earth because Gray Owl is crying," you deserve to lose your home in a global-warming disaster.

Beat.

You know when we'll see movement on climate change?
When forest fires rip through the mansions of Rosedale.

Beat.

They're not laughing as much for that one down here in the expensive seats.

Beat.

It's not that bad.
That poster in my elementary school is not that bad.
Exotification isn't that bad.
It's racism, but it's not the worst kind of racism.
In fact, it's probably the best kind of racism.

Beat.

Once, when I was a young man, there was a woman who, at the end of a date, invited me to stay and . . . *behave* like a wolf.

Beat.

I was so offended . . .
But "Owooooo."

Beat.

It's simple.
Stories are supposed to be simple.
Easy to understand.
The Earth is our mother.
Everyone should think like that.

Beat.

Here's the problem with thinking like that:
Some Indigenous people don't care about the environment.
Or they do but they don't care about the environment more than anyone else.
Or they do, but you'd never be able to tell by their actions.

Beat.

Just like everyone else.

Beat.

I'm sure there are Indigenous people out there who separate their plastics and call it a day.
What about the conservative Indian?
Works a trade.
Takes care of his family.
Doesn't like being told what to do.

Beat.

Oh, that's not the Indigenous voice we should be listening to at this time.
It's some other Indigenous voice a little more in step with my beliefs.

Beat.

What is the point of telling you that not all Indigenous people are conscientious members of the global community . . . because the views of Indigenous people vary as widely as the views of any people.
When you invoke Indigeneity as a means to an end, you're not fighting for us, you're using us as a pawn.

Beat.

And here's the thing: a lot of times, I agree with you.
I see your point; I hold your opinion; I share your view, but when you use my cultural identity for one of your little victories, I feel stereotyped.

I don't like to feel stereotyped.

Beat.

Save a whale, club a seal, keep me out of it.

Beat.

White people, do you want me to look at the colour of your skin
and assume . . . your peckerwood ass hails from the boonies of West
Virginia and you masturbate to concentration camp porn cloaked in a
Confederate flag?

Beat.

Well, I've heard that's what you all are like.

Beat.

No, here's what I think of you.
You have a lot of money in the bank.

Beat.

You have so much money in the bank that you could not work this
month—you'd be okay.
In fact, you could not work this month, go on vacation, hit your house pay-
ment, and you'd be okay.
I think you've never experienced any kind of mental illness . . . but maybe
someone in your family has.
I think you've never been to prison . . . and maybe *no one* in your family has.
I think that you have a dispenser in your fridge that distributes water.

Beat.

You've got crystal glassware, sterling silver dining ware, and you're a
Protestant.

Beat.

In fact ... United.

Beat.

How'd I do?

Beat.

Zero?
No one?

Beat.

The guy with the money is like, yeah you got me.

Beat.

No, stereotypes aren't real.
I don't want to be your stereotype either, even if it's a gee-golly-whiz-great
stereotype like: Indigenous person, steward of the environment.
That's annoying.
Not the worst.
You know what, seriously, keep doing it.
I like it better than when you throw driveshafts at us from moving car
windows.

Beat.

I have suffered—and life is suffering, isn't it ladies and gentlemen?
Life is suffering...
I don't want to get into it, but I have even suffered racial discrimination.
I know what you're thinking: "Of course you have, you stupid fuckin'
Indian."

Beat.

"You're being discriminated against right now."

Beat.

But you don't say it.
For that, I'm grateful to be a Canadian.

Beat.

Canada Day is coming.
Do you know what you're going as?

Beat.

Now let me tell you a good reason to link Indigenous people to the environmental movement.
Our stories live in the land.
Our history lives in the land.
I visited my family in Patuanak.
In northern Saskatchewan wild blueberries are of great cultural significance.
We picked spots my family has known for generations.
Along the way, certain rocks or trees or divergences in the path would unlock a story from my uncle.
Down here is where the mine was.
That's where so and so died.
Here's where we got a moose one year when we needed one.
This is where your aunty and I had our first date.
This is a man who doesn't say two words for the rest of the day.
Something about going to these places pulls the story out of him.
If we didn't visit these places there'd be no reason to tell these stories, so if the land is lost our history is lost.
Acknowledge that.

Beat.

I want to know: Do people of money and influence hear a land acknowledgement and then turn their head to support an environmental cause?

Do they hire an Indian?

Beat.

I don't think so.
It's not a very wealth-friendly message.
Aren't I saying that your wealth and trappings came from something other
than hard work?

Beat.

And they did.
They did.
Come on.
You know how I know?
You know how I know you didn't get all this because of hard work: straw-
berry pickers work a lot harder than you.

Beat.

Must be because you're so smart?

Beat.

Smart enough not to be a strawberry picker?

Beat.

I'm afraid rich people hear a land acknowledgement, nod in approval, and
then wait patiently for their show to begin.
Which, by the way, is what's about to happen to you.
I'm going to wrap up my little land acknowledgement and then you'll have
it *As You Like It*.
But no, I'm with you: I'd be disinclined to entertain the notion that I am an
unworthy recipient of my home and talent.

Beat.

Unless of course . . . I was an "ally."
You know, an ally who is philosophically opposed to himself.

Beat.

He loudly trumpets marginalized voices but doesn't bother volunteering at the
Native centre—and have you heard this: a lot of allies are sexual predators.

Beat.

I didn't say "all."

Beat.

It's probably like sixty percent.

Beat.

No, here's the problem with allies.
You feel the need to call yourselves allies.
You announce yourself to the world as anti-racist, blindly pro-whatever
your friends of colour say.
Is that a problem?
Well, it's obnoxious, but is it a problem?
Yes.
Because we need you covert.
We need you inside the businesses and institutions.
We need people to trust you with their prejudices.
Listen for this clue: "We're both white guys here, right?"

Beat.

Maybe I'm wrong.
Because it's serious out there.
It's a war out there.
We can't just be friends.
You can break up with your friends.

You hold fast with your allies even when you're not friends.
Being an ally doesn't mean we barbecue together.
It means we go to war together.

Beat.

Right?
War?
That's the solution to the algorithm.
That's what's at the end of the echo chamber.
West Bank.
You know a lot of people would love to do something like that here.
A lot of people would love to see violent civil war on Canadian soil.
You know who: probably the whole world.

Beat.

Fear, violence, despair is the message of our social-justice allies.

Beat.

But also . . . justice.
We oppose fascism.
We oppose bigotry.
We stand united against homophobia, transphobia.
We stand united in non-violence.
We stand against hate.

Beat.

What about Nazis?

Beat.

Do we hate Nazis?

Beat.

Are we allowed to be violent towards Nazis?

Beat.

Yes.
No.
I don't know.
I just go along with whatever my friends think is cool.

Beat.

What is an ally?
What does an ally do, besides post a hashtag?
Does your ally give you a job?
Maybe.
What is an ally?
I went online and checked out some left wing, academic sloganeering.

Beat.

What an ally does is: one, educate oneself about different identities and experiences.
Two, challenge one's own discomfort and prejudice—you know, don't be an asshole.

Beat.

Three, learn and practise the skills of being an ally . . . so run one and two.
Four—here it is: having had a spiritual awakening as a result of these steps . . . take action to create interpersonal, institutional, and societal change.
Steps one through three are great.
They're great.
They help one realize one is not the only person in the goddamn world.

Beat.

Step four, now that you realize you're not the only person in the goddamn world, you're ready to make some changes around here.

Beat.

Okay, my ally, what have you changed?
Interpersonally.
And do not tell me you pushed an old person around your family dinner table.
Don't tell me you cornered your father about some belief he cultivated in 1957 and badgered him until he lashed out and used the word "squaw."
That kind of interpersonal change I do not feel benefits the Indigenous community.

Beat.

Also, don't tell me you posted an orange square and you're ready to accept your Nobel Peace Prize.
Posting an orange square doesn't make you a changemaker.
That makes you a trend-follower.
That makes you a virtue-signaller.

Beat.

After interpersonal change . . . let's step right over institutional change.
Because that one's really hard.
You have to work in an institution to make any change there.
That's boring.
Institutional change is for suckers.

Beat.

Let's step right over institutional change and head right for the sexy one: societal change.

Beat.

Come on, Mark Zuckerberg.
Maybe one in a million bring about societal change.
Societal change is unattainable for most of us.
That's why it's more likely that a conservative, rich-ass white motherfucker
is gonna be a better ally than a broke-ass lefty Internet troll.

Beat.

A few more laughs down here for that one . . .

Beat.

It's hard to be a good person.
A truly *good* person.
Good people do good things.
Good things are expensive.
A good person will build a wing on a hospital.
A good person will give you their kidney.
Kidneys are expensive.

Beat.

We throw around these terms like "good person" and "ally" to anyone who
clicks subscribe.
Using the term "ally" sounds like you're fighting Nazis in World War II.
And you're not.
You're fighting for likes on Facebook.

Beat.

You want me to acknowledge:
"Ally" . . . it's your thing, man.
It's got nothing to do with me.
You can't be my ally because I'm not in a war.

Beat.

Let's be friends.
I'm not talking fake friends—like . . . you colonized their country but you
did a land acknowledgement.

    Beat.

I'm talking: real friends.
A friend, for the purpose of this land acknowledgement, is someone whose
work supports your own, either because they care about you or believe in
what you're doing.
You have to work together.
Let's use the term "work" loosely.
It doesn't have to mean we did some deal on the golf course.

    Beat.

Were you relieved just then?

    Beat.

When I said you don't have to golf with me.

    Beat.

No, let's use the term "work" loosely.
Listening can be work if the content is difficult to hear.
Watching golf can be work if you don't like golf.
Acknowledging important moments in each other's lives is work.
If you're not doing any work in your friendships, you're probably not a very
good friend.

    Beat.

Don't be an ally.
Be a friend.

    Beat.

I have gotten off track.
Well, I don't want to take full responsibility.
I was triggered.

Beat.

Allies are one of my triggers.

Beat.

The point I'm trying to make is . . . I don't think a land acknowledgement is a direct appeal to the "haves."

Beat.

I'm not saying to the great white father: "Oh please, Daddy, stick that Molson Canadian up my brown ass a little bit harder and a little bit deeper."

Beat.

Anyone here drink Molson Canadian?

Beat.

It might taste a little different this May two-four.

Beat.

No, must be a message to the middle class.
We must gather together as small fish to take on the big fish?

Beat.

Mmm.
I don't know.
I don't know that the prevailing sentiment of the middle class is that you are akin with the Indigenous.

Fellow small fish to be ganged up with.
Are we a team?

Beat.

I don't know.
And it's not because you're all hung up on your misinterpretations of
tax law.
You think Indians all got a free ride and we're still complaining.

Beat.

Are you?

Beat.

Are you?
Do we have to go back there?
Do we have to cover tax law in this land acknowledgement?
Okay we will.

Beat.

But we'll do it at the end, like an appendix.
Or an encore, if you will.

Beat.

I want to know if we're a team.
Let's find out.
Let's play a game.
Let's play a game.
Show of hands, nice and loose, and remember: there are no wrong answers.

Beat.

First question: How many of you know who Elijah Harper is?

Beat.

You know what, that was too hard.
That's too hard for the first question.
But let's call that homework.
I would love if you knew who Elijah Harper is by the time we stage *All's Well That End's Well.*

Beat.

Next question: How many of you know who Jody Wilson-Raybould is?

Beat.

Who is he?

Beat.

That's right, *she* was the Minister of Justice, and the only one of us to meaningfully tell Justin Trudeau to go fuck himself.

Beat.

How many of you have read a book by an Indigenous author?

Beat.

How many of you have listened to an album by an Indigenous musician?

Beat.

For everyone who hasn't, check out Cris Derksen's *Orchestral Powwow.*
I'm hooking you up right now.
I don't get anything for saying that.

Beat.

How many of you have watched a movie or TV show by and about Indigenous people.
Reservation Dogs counts.

Beat.

North of 60 counts.

Beat.

I even think *Trickster* counts.

Beat.

This is going really well.
We may just be a team.
Next question: How many of you have had an Indigenous person in your home?

Beat.

Now, they didn't *work* for you . . .

Beat.

Okay, for everyone who just admitted that, no, you've never had an Indigenous person into your home: thank you for being honest.
You're honest people.

Beat.

You're not friends of the Indigenous community.

Beat.

But I don't think we should cancel you.

Beat.

For everyone else who purport to having an Indigenous person in your home—

Beat.

How many of you celebrate Christmas with an Indigenous family?

Beat.

Oh, you're breaking my heart.

Beat.

So, are we a team?
Sure, sure we are.
But we're like . . . a bar-league softball team: you don't always have to show up.

Beat.

I have one more question, and this one is for any immigrants in the house who feel like playing.
I want to know if we share this:
Has a white person ever come up to you and said: "It's just awful what we've done to your people"?
"I mean, historically."
"It's just terrible what we've done to your people." Have they?

Beat.

That has happened to me many times.

Beat.

You know why he says that?

He says that because it makes him feel better.

Beat.

He knows he's not as low down as me.
He's grateful he's not the bottom rung.
That's gratitude, right.
That's what that word gratitude means.

Beat.

That's what I think when I see white guys doing land acknowledgements.

Beat.

Indigenous people doing land acknowledgements . . . is even worse.
I hate it.
I hate seeing an Indigenous person stand up here and say they were born a victim.
I hate it.

Beat.

Now.
Land acknowledgements didn't begin as left-wing academic sloganeering.
They began as whispers around kitchen tables in the seventies.
They began as a dare.

Beat.

What if we told them.

Beat.

What if we told them.

Beat.

What if we walked right into their house.

Beat.

Said it, right to their face: all this shit . . . you stole it.

Beat.

You stole it.

Beat.

Your family lied, cheated, extorted, stole, and laughed.
They fucking laughed.

Beat.

You hear that?

Beat.

Silence.

Beat.

No one is laughing now.

Beat. Beat. Beat.

I don't care.
I don't.
I don't care.
That's my defence to it all.
I don't care.
I'm Indian.
I've learned not to get too attached to people, places, things . . . also verbs.

Beat.

I'm grateful.
For example, I love this brief little speck of time—this place where meaning exists.
Think about how small we are.
Humanity is a blip on a timeline.
If you pulled a string from here to the north pole, humanity would be the size of a neutron's taint.

Beat.

We're a fluke.
I am awestruck that radiation from the sun has allowed 4.5 billion earth years to slip by, evolving bipedal apes ordering different combinations on our sandwiches and cable packages.

Beat.

Awestruck.

Beat.

We're so new.
All this, be good to each other and get along, we just came up with that.
We're still learning and growing.
Practising.
But we got a long way to go.
Human beings do some pretty terrible things to each other.

Beat.

For every miracle vaccine a million murderers walk free.

Beat.

Fact-check that.

That seems like a lot.
I hope that's not true.

Beat.

You know what I mean.
For every lost pet safely returned home—another is chained to the radiator, getting whooped with a TV antenna.

Beat.

No, humanity is not the ultimate good.

Beat.

I want to ask you something.
Do you care about your ancestors?

Beat.

You had ancestors who died horrible deaths in fear, too young after losing many children.
Imagine this . . . your great-great-great-great-great-great-great-great-great-great-great-great grandmother was a single mom . . . living on welfare.

Beat.

Your great-great-great-great-great-great-great-great-great-great-great-great grandfather was a drunken adulterer, didn't give a fuck.
She was a slave and she worked in the fields every day until she collapsed and died there.
Now I wanna know . . . do you feel bad for her?

Beat.

You're giving me nothing right now.
You don't trust me?

I've been up here for forty-five minutes, giving this land acknowledgement, and now you're gonna act like we're strangers?
Do you feel bad for her?

Beat.

Did anyone say "no"?
That's cold.
You don't care about your great-great-great-great-great-great-great-great-great-great-great-great grandmother?

Beat.

But the rest of us . . . "yes."
Right?
Of course.

Beat.

Come on, you didn't even know her.

Beat.

She's not even real.

Beat.

I made her up.
I made her up to prove a point to you.
Does anyone remember what it was?

Beat.

Oh yeah.
I fabricated a terrible tragedy to win some social moment.
And it was so easy.
Did you get into it?

Were you like, "Yeah, I'm from an oppressed people too."

Beat.

Of course you are.
You are.
The real story is far worse than anything I could come up with.
In fact, I'd like to acknowledge at this time: history has been unkind to the Irish.

Beat.

But let's move on.

Beat.

Because history has been unkind to everyone.
The Irish.
The Jews.
The Irish Jews.
Blacks, Indians, gays, women, immigrants, Haitians, Croatians, Chechens, Serbians, Bosnians, South Africans, Kenyans, Ugandans, Rwandans, Palestinians, the Rohingya Muslims, the Toronto Maple Leafs.

Beat.

Who hasn't history been unkind to?
Oh, you know who?
The rich, that's who.
I have two science questions that I hope can be responsibly answered by two contradictory scientific opinions.
This is for the land acknowledgement.

Beat.

This protest is turning into a blockade, isn't it?

Beat.

I have two science questions that I hope can be responsibly answered by
two contradictory scientific opinions.
I'd like to welcome two different scientists to the stage, not too singular and
odd-looking.

Beat.

Bring me Neil deGrasse Tyson.
Don't bring me Stephen Hawking.

Beat.

And don't bring me an Indigenous female scientist either.
Because . . . you're not ready for that.

Beat.

You're not.
You're not ready to accept a female Indigenous scientist's opinion as
separate from her cultural identity.
That's advanced race relations.

Beat.

That's not you.
That's not your fault either.
I'll tell you why: when you see a white guy on stage, he could be anyone.
From president to serial killer and everything in between.
We have seen it all.
There's context.
You'll need to see a female Indigenous . . . mass shooter before you're ready
for a female Indigenous scientist.

Beat.

Okay, we're going to ask two scientists two questions and then vote on who's hotter.

Beat.

First question: Is blood memory real?
Are you infested by the pain of your ancestors?
Do the injustices inflicted upon your great-great-great-great-great-great-great-great-great-great-great-great grandmother resonate with you at this moment?

Beat.

Part B: If "yes," is that pain exacerbated by seeing all these white mother-fuckers out here with shit you don't have?

Beat.

Hold on now, it's not just blood memory.
It's learned behaviours passed down from one generation to another.
Let me ask you something ... you're making a Bundt cake.

Beat.

How do you make your Bundt cake?

Beat.

Like your grandma.
Right?

Beat.

That's the same reason you don't get in an elevator with a Black guy.
People's reactions, the reactions of the outside world, shape who we are.
Our environment shapes who we are.
When Grandma doesn't get in the elevator with me, it hurts my feelings.

I think: "What a racist old bitch."

Beat.

Then maybe, if I'm having a bad day, I might just carry that insult with me. Maybe the next little old lady I see, I may think, just for a second, she's a racist old bitch just like the first.

Beat.

Woah.
Of course I'll check myself.
I'll think: "Be cool, man."
She's just a little old lady.
She probably marched with Elijah Harper.

Beat.

I check myself, but it doesn't matter.
She saw that flash of anger in my eye.
And she's scared.
Aww.
And she gets angry when she gets scared.
And Grandma Karen calls the police when she gets angry.

Beat.

We are in a one-hundred-fifty-year toxic relationship.
From dirty looks to bad vibes to incarceration to murder.

Beat.

I don't blame you.

Beat.

I blame the system.

Beat.

The system some of you orchestrate like a virtuoso composer.

Beat.

Ah, don't blame the system, man.
The system's just there for us all to get along.
No, it's there for you to get along.
It's there to put my ass in prison.

Beat.

(runs) But ... Creator loves us.
Creator loves us.
You know how I know?
You tried to kill us.
So many times.
Poisonous chemicals in the river, can't touch this.
Dietary diabetes, pour some sugar on me.
Murder by the police, we're still here.
Creator loves us.

Beat.

But just the same, there are places in this country where Indigenous people
today—and I can't believe I'm talking to you like *National Geographic*—

Beat.

There are places in this country Indigenous people today have been dealt
brutal cards.
Places like Grassy Narrows.
There's mercury in the water.
Fish born with three eyes.
Cancer at young ages.
Spider babies.

Beat.

Okay, not spider babies.

Beat.

I was kidding about spider babies . . . but stay tuned.

Beat.

Attawapiskat.
There's a housing shortage.
A suicide epidemic.
There are people who would rather die than live in Canada with you.

Beat.

In English River First Nation.
Uranium mines have contaminated the water.
It's an environmental disaster—or what the Dene call "home."

Beat.

Oh, by the way, it's my responsibility to acknowledge our sponsors.
Tonight's presentation is brought to you by TD, RBC, and Scotiabank.

Beat.

Grassy Narrows, Attawapiskat, and English River First Nation.

Beat.

Acknowledge also that land acknowledgements are a protest for representation.
There need to be more Indians represented in our educational institutions, in the medical system, in the judicial system—

Well ... I suppose we have enough Indians represented in the judicial system, don't you?

Beat.

We have so many Black and Brown men in prison.
I, myself, have three brothers who have served time in prison.
But!
One of them was Irish.

Beat.

He was adopted.

Beat.

Please keep up.

Beat.

Let's acknowledge, however: Indigeneity is not the answer for everything.
There are Indians who think we have hidden secrets in every field.
Indigenous physics, Indigenous mathematics, Indigenous theatre.

Beat.

I don't know ... they may not be wrong.
You can't blame these Indians for trying.
You stole our culture.
We're taking it back piece by piece.

Beat.

Let's talk fur for a second.

Beat.

I don't mean the raccoon in your Hudson's Bay hat.

Beat.

When European ancestors came pullin' in here shivering, starving, diseased—

Beat.

Pasty.

Beat.

What were they given?
They were given meat and fur.

Beat.

The fur trade is the economy this country was founded upon.
Have you ever tanned a hide before?
If you haven't but you wear fur, shame on you.
If you have, you know it is brutally difficult work.
All day, in the sun.
Our Indigenous women are hardened to that work.
That work is a sacred gift passed from generation through generation and
handed to you by these women.
How has that most divine act of generosity been acknowledged, with over
four thousand murdered and missing Indigenous women and girls.
My sisters are endangered, you motherfuckers.

Beat.

When my sister goes to the store, I say: "Hold on, I'll go with you."

Beat.

You know where to get some fur?

I mean where the dope shit is at.

Beat.

Don't go to fashion week.
Go to Indigenous fashion week.
You can get the most beautiful garments, the most stunning jewellery, and the most eccentric wearable designs.
You put your money in the hand of the person who made it.
How's that for fast fashion.

Beat.

Many of our designers are reclaiming stolen practices and giving them a contemporary context, which is . . . hot.
Best of all, you'll have pieces that your basic bitch HBC friends don't have.

Beat.

By the way, it's been great watching that company slowly die.

Beat.

Okay, what are we forgetting to acknowledge?
What are we forgetting to acknowledge?
What would we love to overlook?

Beat.

The bodies of over seven thousand residential school children have turned up in unmarked gravesites across the country.
Children who would've been alive today were they not murdered.
The community is crying out.
And they knew it.
They knew it like it was a dream.
"There are kids buried in those hills."
No one believed them.

Some probably didn't want to believe themselves.
Noises in the night.
The next day: one less classmate.
One less sibling.
No messages were sent home.
Children probably had to tell the parents who they'd lost.
Imagine: going down to pick up your child at the end of semester, finally, and they're not on the bus.

Beat.

The first school that broke was in Kamloops.
The school operated for eighty years.
They reported that fifty-one kids died there, but new bullshit-detecting equipment turned up more.

Beat.

The Catholic Church—

Shivers.

Did you feel that?

Beat.

The Catholic Church has been asked to turn over records and they said:
"Absolutely."

Beat.

Then give us the records.
"Of course."
Let's have the records.
"Certainly."
Give us the records.
"Your call is important to us, please hold."

Beat.

Come on, even the Germans kept records.

Beat.

Did they not keep records because they didn't want anyone to find out what they'd done?
Was it because they were lazy, like, "Damn I just killed and buried an Indian kid, you want me to write about it too."
Did they not care?
Like, you don't write down every time you cut down a tree or eat a fish.
Why would you write down every time you kill an Indian.

Beat.

When I first heard, I was hit with a lot of questions.
How many feet from the back door was the site?
How might the site have been selected?
Was it selected for secrecy or convenience?
Was there evidence of Catholic ritual?
With no evidence of Catholic ritual, how did the child murderers know where and where not to dig, year after year?
Who buried the dead kids?
How'd they die?
I thought we should know how each of them died: was it disease?
Starvation?
Did they freeze?
Were they killed in sexual assault?
I thought we should know for each child.
I think when something terrible happens you pick up each piece of evidence, label it, ask: How could this happen?
The pieces of a genocide are . . . blood, hair, teeth, and thousands of tiny shoes.

Beat.

The community decided not to exhume the bodies.
Which is a relief.

Beat.

As far as I'm concerned, officials from the Catholic Church should be living in South America under assumed identities.

Beat.

Any priests here tonight?

Beat.

Is it me or does the image of the Catholic priest need to be rebranded?
I only see "pedophile."
With their foreskin collar and flowing pedophile robes.
I know what you did to that altar boy back there.
I don't need evidence, I know.

Beat.

I saw a priest the other day.
He was cruising around in a GT and sunglasses.
I said, "Father, is it hard to maintain humility in the presence of all this bounty?"
He smiles, like he doesn't give a fuck, and goes: "I try."

Beat.

Did you hear about the priest who got the Indian girl pregnant and then threw her baby in the furnace?

Beat.

I can't remember the punchline so I guess we'll just have to carry it like that.

Beat.

To be honest, I feel a solidarity with these kids.
Why?
I wasn't murdered.
I didn't attend residential school.
To be honest, I'm a very privileged person.

Beat.

I'll tell you why, as it was explained to me.
My generation is the first generation to have parents as parents.
Generations of Indians were raised in these schools.
Let's stop calling them schools tonight, shall we.
Let's call them what they are.
Camps.
They're not concentration camps—because the showers sprayed water.

Beat.

They're not internment camps.

Beat.

No, we had rape camps.
Kids were sent to have their culture raped from them.

Beat.

My tenth-grade history teacher told me that the road to hell is paved with good intentions.

Beat.

Does that sound fucking stupid to anyone else?
The intentions were not good.
The intentions were to kill the Indian in the child.

Those graves were unmarked.
Unmarked graves.

Beat.

That's proof they never wanted us as Catholics.

Beat.

Maybe some individual teachers were good . . . I mean Robert Mugabe was a cat lover.

Beat.

Maybe there were good nuns, which—

Laughs.

Beat.

I'm sorry, if you've ever been rendered powerless by a screaming nun at five years old, you know: this organization will let anyone in.

Beat.

What's it got to do with now.
Aside from breaking the hearts of an entire people.
What's it got to do with now, besides Indigenous life expectancy being lower than the national average.
I get less time than you.
What's it got to do with now?
I'm so glad you asked.
Let's look at reserve school teachers today.
Yeah, let's examine our allies.
Reserve school teachers are made up primarily of young, inexperienced teachers.
No one will hire them in their preferred communities, so they go to the rez to gain experience.

Beat.

They stay in the nicest trailer.
They make the most money.
And the whole time they're there, they think: "See. I'm a good person."
"I'm, like, actually doing something."

Beat.

They stay for two years—LinkedIn profile up the whole time.
Then they fuck off to wherever experienced teachers go.
And they tell their cocktail stories about what an amazing experience it was.

Beat.

But people always want to know more, right.
"Wasn't it really bad?"
"I've heard those places are really bad."
Then, the teacher gets all saucy and goes . . .
(sip) "There was this one time—" and they recount whatever gruesome
image is at the end of their tragedy-porn scale.
The listener is shocked, as they'd hoped, and confirmed what they knew all
along: "Yep, those places are really bad."
"And this teacher . . . one of the good ones."
What a beautiful story.

Beat.

Here's what's wrong with that story.
Teaching is really hard.
It's really hard.
You're just as likely to confuse as you are to clarify.
You're just as likely to damage a student as you are to enrich them.
Teaching is a profession.
It deserves a lifetime of practise.
A great teacher can change someone's future and a worthless flake will ruin
someone's life.

If you've been teaching for less than five years, you suck at it.
If you're in denial about that, you are dangerous.
Canada, all my relations, we live on a land with a history of residential schools, and Indigenous communities are still a dumping ground for the teachers you don't want.

Beat.

So . . . teachers with reserve school experience, you ain't shit.
You ain't shit.
Probably.
Just painting by the numbers here.
But!
Your image is not beyond rehabilitation.
Here's what you can do.
Come back to the reserve when you're actually a good teacher.
After you've made your humiliating newbie mistakes.
Once you are that wise old sage bringing the elusive threads of the unknown into graspable perspective without poisoning the lesson with your shitty personality.
Come back to the reserve when you're comfortable in your house and school and your chosen community.
Come back when you truly are a gift of a teacher.
Come back then and teach at our schools, serve our community, then I would love to hear your stories, man.
I think they'd be very interesting.
Until then, shut the fuck up.

Beat.

Oh, I shouldn't be too hard on the cocktail party teacher.
Their heart's in the right place.
They're well-intentioned graduates from the university of Ryerson.

Beat.

You heard that, right?

The architect of residential schools, up until very recently, had his name on an institution in my city.

Well, I say that—it wasn't quite that.

Really what it was, was that he created a mechanism of genocide that was deployed a generation after he died.

He wasn't there with the blueprints going, "Ze children will enter from ze souss side, ya."

Beat.

It wasn't exactly Adolf Eichmann U.

But close enough.

Just saying the syllables left the metallic taste of blood in everyone's mouth.

We made that school change its fucking name.

Beat.

I think, if you legalize marijuana, you should let the marijuana criminals out of jail.

Similarly, if you illegalize genocide on Indians, you take the statues of the murderers down.

Beat.

Well . . . I don't want to be controversial . . .

Beat.

God, would this guy shut up.

You tell me: at what point are we finished acknowledging the abduction and murder of over seven thousand school-aged children?

In fact, I got a good mind to bring out a skid full of thousands of reems of paper that is the entire inquiry and just fucking read it to you—all night— until I lose my voice.

And if anyone wants to leave, they have to stand up in front of everyone and walk out during the land acknowledgement.

Beat.

Let's acknowledge something else: you're not gonna see the show you paid for.

Beat.

As You Like It . . . I've never even read it.
This is a facade.
Open this curtain.

Beat.

This is the show.
The land acknowledgement is your show.

Beat.

I lied to you.

Beat.

I lied to you and took your money.

Beat.

How's it feel?

Beat.

Now you know what it's like to be Indian . . . for a day.

Beat.

If anyone feels duped and disrespected, the bard's sacred texts didn't ring out again tonight, by all means, you can walk out this door and you can get your money back.

I don't want an unearned dollar off the Crow's Theatre audience.
But if you're still with me, let's keep acknowledging.
Acknowledge this: all those pedophile priests and child-molesting nuns
are dead.
It was a different time.
It was a different time.
No, it was three weeks ago.

Beat.

Bodies are still being uncovered.
Things from a different time have a way of maintaining precedent today.
The honorable Murray Sinclair estimates that of the 139 government-run
rape camps there are still twenty thousand children left to be uncovered.
If you factor in the over one hundred thousand privately contracted rape
camps, that number skyrockets.
Where's our Nuremberg?

Beat.

Some of those priests and nuns are still alive.
They can be touched.
If the middle class wasn't so sentimental.
But they haven't been yet because the Catholic Church is an organization
full of cowards.
A pedophile turns up and they ship them away.
They bring South American bishops and cardinals here because, hey, they
had nothing to do with our genocide.
I say they do.
By turning up and putting a good face on the Catholic pedophile cult,
you're enabling genocide retroactively.

Beat.

You know what allies we need . . .
A forensic detective.
A forensic accountant.

... And a dirty cop.

Beat.

I'm talking some French Canadian bacon.

Beat.

Where's a white saviour when you need one?

Beat.

Raid the bishop's house, four a.m., no knock.

Beat.

Pull him out of bed in his underwear.
Seize his hard drives.
Handcuff him on the curb in front of his neighbours for an hour.
Even if he doesn't really have shit—like if it's just to fuck with him.
What?
Such brutal miscarriages of justice occur every day in my community.
How come a high-ranking member of the Catholic Church never turns up
on the news with a fractured skull and a resisting arrest charge?

Beat.

Or frozen to death in the north end of Saskatoon.

Beat.

One ornate slipper.

Beat.

Hasn't happened yet.
You know why?

Because there is no justice.
Not for Indigenous people.
The playing field is not level.

Beat.

Did you hear that the RCMP is investigating the Catholic Church?

Beat.

Think about that.
The RCMP is investigating the Catholic Ch—
That's like if Ross committed a murder and Rachel was sent to investigate.

Beat.

They're friends.

Beat.

Here's something funny.
The group who ran forty-seven percent of the rape camps were called the Missionary Oblates of Mary Immaculate.
They still exist.
That is shocking to me.
I checked out their website.

Beat.

They sidestep some of the important language that I advocate for, words like "genocide," "rape," and "pedophile cult."
Which, how do you discuss the Missionary Oblates without using the term "pedophile cult"?
Kind of a high wire, right?

Beat.

The website does admit that they participated in systems that contribute to the problems that have beset the Native community.
Problems like alcoholism and poverty . . .
These savages, these lowdown kiddie snatchers are still skulking around developing nations like Kenya and Rwanda.
You know what they're doing?
They're setting up schools.

Beat.

They're setting up schools.

Beat.

I don't think the pedophile cult should be allowed to work with children.

Beat.

Too far?

Beat.

I shouldn't be too hard on them.
They're little old people.
They're little old people.
Most of them are well past retirement age.
They go to some far-off locations with their friends and try to spread a little bit of good.

Beat.

They're probably not orchestrating a pedophile ring now—you know what, I'm not gonna say that.
That's too much.
If your aging parent was a hazard to other drivers on the road, you'd make them stop driving.

Please, if your mom or dad is a volunteer warrior in an ongoing cultural genocide, take their keys.

"Say, Mom, you're very confused. I want you to come into the house where it's nice and warm and stop persecuting Indigenous children."

Beat.

Did you hear that Trudeau is very hurt?

Beat.

As a Catholic.
He's still a Catholic.
After all this.
I wanna say, Justin, fuck your Catholicism.

Beat.

All your cozy Sunday-school memories are absolutely corrupt.
You'd shine your shoes and put on your suit and tell your lies of do unto others.
That communion wafer wasn't the symbolic flesh of Christ.
You were symbolically eating the flesh of Indians.
They tortured children in electric chairs.

Beat.

If Costco tortured children in electric chairs, you'd give up your membership to Costco.

Beat.

Not Justin.
He'd keep eating those triple-A Kirkland rib-eyes.
(eats steak) It's time to turn the page on this troublesome chapter with Indigenous people.

Beat.

Alberta premier Jason Kenney made an impassioned plea on behalf of the legacy of John A. Macdonald, founding prime minister, genocidal maniac.

Beat.

He was a monster, but he also did really flaky shit, like widespread fraud, cockeyed gerrymandering—
Even if you're a straight-up racist, a white supremacist, you hate the Indians—and if you are: I congratulate you for making it this far in the land acknowledgement . . .
Even if you're a first-class racist you should be interested in dragging the name John A. through the public square.
He was a seedy pile of human garbage.
His proficiency with certain mechanisms of power is nothing to be proud of.
We only hold him up because of all the statues and signs—and guess what: he put them there.
Let's take 'em down.
Or at least put up new plaques so it says right there, weighted evenly with everything else he did: this guy was a lying murderer.

Beat.

Jason Kenney said that you can't "cancel" history.
I say, "History has been canceled for a long time, Jay."
"Let's schedule a history class."

Beat.

Did you hear the pope apologize?

Beat.

Well I feel much better.

He'll settle with white people for millions of dollars but says "sorry" to us, that racist piece of shit.

Beat.

My granny would be very upset if she heard me say the pope is a racist piece of shit.
So, let me acknowledge . . . there are many Indians who are Catholics.
I get that.
Many people in our community have suffered terrible loss, psychological and physical trauma.
If you've been in that real blackness, it might be nice to believe that your loved ones are in a better place.

Beat.

That when you were in that darkness, you were not alone.
Jesus Christ was there with you.
I get that.
But if you haven't.
Been in that real blackness, and you're still a Catholic because, oh, Grandma was, well you're just stupid.
You colonized motherfucker.

Beat.

Of all the religions that exist you chose the one that committed genocide on your Indigenous brothers and sisters.
That is an insult to history.
Consider Buddhism.

Beat.

By the way, if there are any allies looking to make some societal change, there are plenty of churches to burn down right here.

Beat.

I mean, don't do that.
I don't know what I mean.

Beat.

Are you with me?
Are you making the jumps in logic that link residential schools with the
Catholic Church today?
I'm sure I'm not fully making the case to everybody.
In fact, I'm not sure I'm even making the case to myself.
I haven't checked in in a while.
I can taste blood, and you know what . . . I'm angry.

Beat.

I'm angry.

Beat.

I'm really angry.

Beat.

I've tried to deny my anger.
I've tried to keep it out of the room.
I'll tell you why . . . because I was raised . . . in show business.
Show business is about being liked.
No one likes Mr. Angry Pants
So what I do, is I take all that anger and frustration and just . . . push
it down!
I put on my little Indian suit and my little Indian shoes and walk into that
big audition and do my little Indian dance and walk back out and I say to
myself: I hope they liked me.

Beat.

I hope they liked me.

Beat.

So yeah, I'm angry.

And I'm having a hard time keeping it here.
Aren't you angry?
Aren't you irate?
Aren't you so chartreuse you could just, ugh . . .

Beat.

Write a cheque to the healing lodge and be done with it?

Beat.

Please do.
Don't not write a cheque to the healing lodge because I'm a jackal.

Beat.

In fact, there is a trauma-informed counsellor here tonight.
I'm serious.
No one signed up for this experience.
So maybe you're shaking with anger and you need a moment to calm down
before operating a motor vehicle.
Or maybe you'd just like to have a quiet chat away from the bar.
It's either Cheryl or Jodi, depending on who's night it is, and either of these
Indigenous healers, you can look them in the eye and you know: they've
been there.

Beat.

Obviously you won't find me in the studio after the show.
Not cuz I don't need help.
I do need help, listen to me.

Beat.

I just don't trust anyone to help me.
Wait, you want to help me regulate my emotions?
Get me better at accepting this shit.
Give me a pill, tuck me in, make me a good little Indian who honors my culture through recycling.

Beat.

I'm already feeling more likeable.

Beat.

I want to end by telling you two stories of the women in my family.
The first woman walks to the corner store with twenty-five cents in her hand hoping to buy one egg for her two kids.

Beat.

That's fucking heart.
That's get-up-and-go.

Beat.

This Indigenous woman, who raised three Dene babies damn near single-handed . . .

Beat.

She's not Indigenous.
She's Hungarian.
She calls herself an ally, but—

Beat.

That's family.
That's the kind of spirit that sets you above.
That makes you one of the people who didn't stand for this shit.

None of this happened on Shawn Gray's watch.
Shawn Gray was holding hers down.

Beat.

Maybe, instead of abolishing the statues of John A., there should be others erected for Shawn Gray.
In direct opposition.

Beat.

Some local governments are investing in remantling the toppled statues.
I think that's great.
Cuz now we know how easy they come down.

Beat.

Thanksgiving is coming.
We've never been sure how to acknowledge that holiday.

Beat.

I was born in Pine Ridge, South Dakota, but I wasn't raised there.
I was raised in Toronto.
My father still lives there.
Every now and again I go back and visit.

Beat.

I have over two thousand family members.
If you ever visit Pine Ridge, South Dakota, everyone looks like me.
I thought I had European features—don't laugh at me.

Beat.

In Pine Ridge, we'll sit together, fifteen people in a room, laughing or crying.

Every now and then we collapse into these silences.

Beat.

Beat.

Beat.

That's Tipi culture.
When there are fifteen Indians living in one room, you learn . . . to shut the fuck up.
That silence is golden.

Beat.

Then when it's time to talk again, everyone gets one in and tries to make everyone laugh.
Pine Ridge, South Dakota, is the poorest place in North America.
We love to make each other laugh.
Sometimes the only thing in the cupboards is laughter.

Beat.

I'll be honest with you: there's a portion of people in my community who are caught up with crystal meth.

Beat.

Don't look at me like that.
There's a portion of people in your home community that are caught up in crystal Meth.

Beat.

No one knows how to treat crystal meth addiction.
Families of addicts all over the world have tried every method under the sun to treat crystal meth addiction.

Everyone tries, no one has the cure.

Beat.

Some families send their kid to rehab.
They clean her up.
Teach her to live life on life's terms.
Then they give her a little chip and send her home to live happily ever after.

Beat.

Then they do it again a few months later.
And again and again and again until the miracle occurs.
Or she dies.

Beat.

Some families: it's tough love.
They say: "I will not support the decisions you're making so I have to turn my back on you."

Beat.

Might be the right thing to do in a given circumstance.

Beat.

My family does things a little differently.
In my family, if your kids don't have any food in their bellies yet your glass pipe heaps—you will answer to the swift justice of Auntie Nita.

Beat.

You won't like that.

Beat.

Auntie Nita is sixty-five.
A spiritual woman.
A sweat-lodge woman.
She wears turquoise rings on each finger of both hands—so when she punches you in the face it rattles your teeth.
She weighs about eighty-seven pounds . . . and it's all in her eyeballs.

Beat.

Auntie Nita is deaf in one ear . . . and in the other ear she don't give a shit.

Beat.

So when you beg and plead and scream that you'll never get high again . . . she just can't hear you.

Beat.

Auntie Nita feeds twenty-seven people three meals a day.
That's how big my family is.

Beat.

Think about how much love you have to have in your heart to feed twenty-seven people three meals a day.
She's been to funerals and teacher conferences for many children.
If there's anyone I trust to deliver that ass beating in a good way . . . it's Auntie Nita.

Beat.

Auntie Nita doesn't roll alone either.
My cousin Carly rides shotgun.
Carly is fifteen years old.
She has had a shit last few years.
I don't want to get into it—she's got some anger to burn off.

Beat.

This day, they're rolling past my cousin Tiffany's place.
Tiffany's daughter, Brittney, hadn't been to school for three days—school called my Auntie Nita.
That's how deep shit rolls on the rez.

Beat.

School doesn't call the police—school calls Auntie Nita.
Auntie Nita gets shit done.

Beat.

Also you just don't call the police on my rez.
You call the police, everyone's in danger.

Beat.

So they cruise over to Tiffany's place.
The doors are wide open.
Dogs are running in and out.
Shards of Tina sit next to the glass pipe on the windowsill.
They open the bedroom door and she's dogfucking her boyfriend, Terrence Jr.
Porno blasting on the TV.
Balls slapping.

Beat. Beat. Beat.

They shut the door.
They head back to the kitchen and find little Brittney standing on a chair at the stove cooking grilled cheese for her and her little brother.

Beat.

Brittney turns and the swelling is going down on a black eye.
Looks like it happened . . . three days ago.

Beat.

Carly takes over grilled-cheese sandwich making.
While Auntie Nita heads back to the bedroom.
She arrives to see Terrence dive out the window while simultaneously sliding his jeans up over his brown ass like an Olympic high jumper.

Beat.

Tiffany's titties are all out and she's screaming about her rights, but Nita pops her a tidy little left hook that wakes Tiffany the fuck up.

Beat.

Tiffany punches Nita from the clinch, but Nita gets the best of her—swings on her with those rings, drops Tiffany like a tobacco offering.
Pow.

Beat.

Ding.
Cousin Carly, fresh from serving three grilled cheese sandwiches,
picks Tiffany back up: "Don't you ever hit Auntie," and beats her ass a second time.

Beat.

That's what I call a community-led safety solution.

Beat.

Let's acknowledge.
First, this approach may not work in every neighbourhood.

Beat.

Second, my cousin Carly is looking for a job.

Beat.

She's good with her hands.

Beat.

I wanted to finish with these stories of these women in my family—Shawn Gray, Auntie Nita, Carly—because they are the spirit that have kept my people alive.
Strong.
Sexy.
Mean.
Your Indigenous friend will tease you to the doorstep of cruelty.
Then a little bit further.

Beat.

Finally, we have a saying, where I come from.
All my relations.
It means: we're all related.
It doesn't mean: we're all related except for the white people.
It means:
We.
Are.
All.
Related.
Family.
We're supposed to be family.
But we're not.
We're not.
We're not.
And it breaks my heart.
It fucking kills me.

Beat.

I'm Cliff Cardinal.
You have witnessed my land acknowledgement.

After the curtain.

Can I just say one thing?

Thanks for checking out *As You Like It* by William Shakespeare.

To that point . . . there's a ruse with this show.

I beseech ye . . .

I implore . . .

Nay beg.

Please don't tell anyone.

We think it's cooler if people show up and are surprised, so by all means tell your friends: go see it.

Or . . . don't go see it.

But any information about the content or the casting, please keep that to yourself.

If you feel inclined to join us in our ruse . . . tell them about the Shakespeare.

Born on the Pine Ridge Indian Reservation, Cardinal (*Stitch*, *Huff*, and *Cliff Cardinal's CBC Special*) studied playwriting at the National Theatre School of Canada, is a playwright-in-residence at Video Cabaret, and fronts Cliff Cardinal & The Sky-Larks. The author thanks his friends Chris and Sherrie and their team at Crow's Theatre.